WHIT'S END

MEALTIME
DEVOTIONS
THE SECOND HELPING

FOCUS ON THE FAMILY PRESENTS

Adventures in
ODYSSEY®

WHIT'S END
MEALTIME DEVOTIONS
THE SECOND HELPING

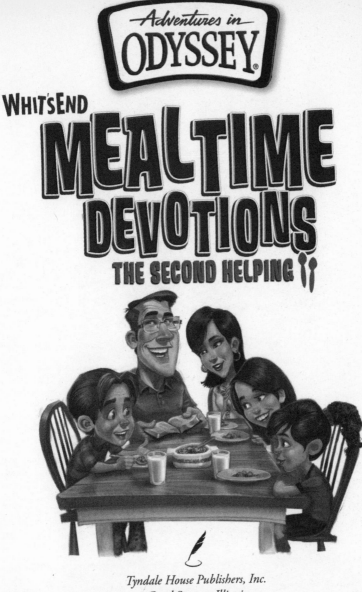

Tyndale House Publishers, Inc.
Carol Stream, Illinois

90 MORE IDEAS YOUR KIDS WILL EAT UP!

JOHN AVERY WHITTAKER
WITH HELP FROM CRYSTAL BOWMAN, TRISHA GOYER, KEVIN MILLER, ED STRAUSS, AND LINDA WURZBACHER

WHIT'S END MEALTIME DEVOTIONS: THE SECOND HELPING
© 2013 Focus on the Family

A Focus on the Family book published by Tyndale House Publishers, Inc., Carol Stream, Illinois 60188

Focus on the Family and Adventures in Odyssey, and the accompanying logos and designs, are federally registered trademarks of Focus on the Family, 8605 Explorer Drive, Colorado Springs, CO 80920.

TYNDALE and Tyndale's quill logo are registered trademarks of Tyndale House Publishers, Inc.

Scripture quotations are taken from the *Holy Bible, New International Version*®, NIV® Copyright © 1973, 1978, 1984 by Biblica, Inc.™ Used by permission of Zondervan. *www.zondervan.com.*

Editor: Marianne Hering
Cover design by Stephen Vosloo
Cover illustration and interior illustrations of characters by Gary Locke
Interior design by Lexie Rhodes

ISBN: 978-1-58997-679-5

The material in this book was originally published in the books *Mealtime Moments,* © 2000 Focus on the Family, and *More Mealtime Moments,* © 2001 Focus on the Family.

Printed in the United States of America
1 2 3 4 5 6 7 8 9 / 18 17 16 15 14 13

For manufacturing information regarding this product, please call (800) 323-9400.

Contents

• • • • • • •

Welcome to the Table

by John Avery Whittaker

In today's busy world, it's rare for families to sit down for a meal together. With school, sports, extracurricular activities, work, church, and so much more, when is everyone ever home at the same time for dinner? The more time that you spend as a family, however, the tighter the bonds and the stronger the foundation for your children. So start with a meal—it doesn't have to be dinner—and use this book to turn mealtimes into lively times for talk and teaching about faith. This book will make starting interesting family conversation as easy as pie.

After announcing the title of the devotion, read the Mealtime Prayer suggestion and then ask your children to pray it together. Then read the Appetizer to whet your appetite for more. Follow it with the Main Course. This contains the "meat" of the section. Once you've given your family something to chew on, it's time for Table Talk. These questions will help your kids think about what they've just learned and enable them to digest it for their daily lives. The questions are suitable for all ages; you can go deeper as your children grow. End with Vitamins and Minerals—a Bible verse that relates to the day's reading and discussion. To get the most out of this book, allow yourself to be *flexible*. You don't have to go through it from cover to cover. You might want to use the table of contents to find a topic that sounds good that day or relates to what you'll be eating.

The point is to turn mealtimes into a fun and enjoyable time of learning about each other. It's about bringing God into every part of our lives. Be sensitive to how your children respond. Allow enough time for them to answer the questions, but don't force conversation if they don't seem interested. That usually isn't a problem with kids, I've found. These readings have been time tested around a few tables—and should stir up animated conversations about the things that really matter.

Let's eat!

In a Pickle?

Mealtime Prayer:

Give thanks to God that He is with us in all situations and will guide and direct our lives.

Appetizer:

Q: What is green and bumpy and red all over?
A: A pickle with a sunburn.

How many kinds of pickles can you name?

Main Course:

Ever gotten yourself into a pickle? Not a bumpy, green pickle, of course, but a difficult situation. What happened? The Bible gives examples of people who got themselves into "pickles" and how God helped them:

- Daniel ended up in a lions' den because he prayed, but God kept the lions from hurting him (Daniel 6).
- Jonah disobeyed God and ended up inside the belly of a big fish (yuck!). He prayed to God, and the fish spit him out (Jonah 2).
- When Paul and Silas were in prison for preaching the gospel, they prayed and sang hymns of praise. God sent an earthquake, and their chains fell off (Acts 16).
- Who deserved their "pickles," and who didn't? Why?

Table Talk:

- How do we sometimes end up in a pickle?
- What did the Bible characters above do to get out of trouble? What should we do?
- Will God help us get out of our pickles? Why or why not?

Vitamins and Minerals:

Is any one of you in trouble? He should pray. Is anyone happy? Let him sing songs of praise. (James 5:13)

Not Like Ice Cream

Mealtime Prayer:

As you thank God for your food today, thank Him that He is eternal and that His love is everlasting.

Appetizer:

Q: Which animal lives the longest?

A: The quahog clam. Some live for more than 400 years.[1]

Who is the oldest person you know?

Main Course:

At the beginning of your meal, place a small scoop of ice cream in a bowl. What happens to the ice cream while you eat your dinner?

Ice cream doesn't last long, does it? Name some other things that don't last very long. Name some things that *do* last for a long time.

The Bible says that God is everlasting. What does that mean? What are some things about God that are everlasting?

Table Talk:

- How does God being everlasting make a difference in our lives?
- How do we know that God will always be alive?
- How are Christians everlasting?

Vitamins and Minerals:

Before the mountains were born or you brought forth the earth and the world, from everlasting to everlasting you are God. (Psalm 90:2)

---

1. Jennifer Viegas, "Top 10 Longest Living Animals," *Discovery News*, July 21, 2010, http://news.discovery.com/animals/top-10-longest-living-animals.htm.

Let's Go Fishin'

Mealtime Prayer:
Ask God for opportunities to share your faith and bring others to Him.

Appetizer:
Name all the ways that it is possible to catch fish.

Main Course:
Have you ever gone fishing? If so, what bait did you use? How many fish did you catch? Imagine you caught 500 in an hour. How could it have happened? Read the story of an exciting fishing trip in Luke 5:5–7.

Table Talk:
- How did the men catch so many fish?
- How are people like fish?
- What did Jesus mean when He told the disciples they would catch men?
- What kind of bait can you use when you fish for people?
- Where can you go fishing for people?

Vitamins and Minerals:
"Come, follow me," Jesus said, "and I will make you fishers of men." (Matthew 4:19)

Aromatherapy

Mealtime Prayer:
Ask God to help your life be a sweet smell—pure and acceptable to Him.

Appetizer:
Have each person share his or her favorite smell. Which do you prefer: the smell of food or the smell of flowers? Why?

Main Course:
Why do you enjoy pleasant aromas? What aromas remind you of certain things or events from your life?

The Bible tells us that God enjoys pleasant aromas too. When Noah came out of the ark and offered a sacrifice, "the LORD smelled the pleasing aroma" (Genesis 8:21).

Imagine that your life is an aroma, and everything you do and say is part of your aroma. What would your life aroma be like? Why?

Table Talk:
- If kindness had an aroma, what would it smell like? Why?
- How do you think God feels when you send pleasing aromas to Him?
- How can you make your life smell nice?

Vitamins and Minerals:
We are to God the aroma of Christ among those who are being saved and those who are perishing. (2 Corinthians 2:15)

Sweet Attitudes

Mealtime Prayer:
Ask God to help you be what He wants you to be.

Appetizer:
Do you know how bees make honey? They eat pollen, mix it with their saliva, and put it in their honeycombs![1] Think of as many words as you can that rhyme with the word *bee*.

Main Course:
Why do people use the phrase "busy as a bee"? What do bees do that keeps them so busy?

Every bee has a special job, and each bee does what it's supposed to do without grumbling or complaining. Do you think they have "sweet attitudes"? (Imagine a bee complaint box. What might it contain?)

The teachings in Matthew 5:3–12 are called the Beatitudes or "Bee-attitudes! Read what these verses have to say about attitudes.

Table Talk:
- What does the word *blessed* mean?
- How can you be happy when you are having problems?
- How can changing your attitude help you to be happy instead of sad or angry?
- How can you turn a disaster into an adventure?

Vitamins and Minerals:
Blessed is he who trusts in the LORD. (Proverbs 16:20)

---

1. College of Agricultural and Life Sciences, University of Wisconsin-Madison, "How Bees Make Honey," June 4, 2012, http://news.cals.wisc.edu/departments/highlights/2012/06/04/how-bees-make-honey-producing-honey-is-a-strenuous-team-effort-for-bees/.

Free Refills

Mealtime Prayer:
Think of ways that God provides your family with what you need. Thank Him for providing these things for you.

Appetizer:
Set a pitcher of water on the table. Have everyone guess how many glasses the pitcher of water will fill. Then fill as many glasses as possible. Whose guess was the closest?

Main Course:
Read the story of a poor widow in 2 Kings 4:1–7.

Why did the oil stop when all the jars were full? What do you think would have happened if she had collected more jars? If the widow had come to you for jars, how many would you have given her?

Table Talk:
- How does God provide for poor people today? How can you be part of that?
- How does God provide for you?
- How is the widow's oil like God's blessings?

Vitamins and Minerals:
Now to him who is able to do immeasurably more than all we ask or imagine, according to his power that is at work within us, to him be glory in the church and in Christ Jesus throughout all generations, for ever and ever! Amen. (Ephesians 3:20–21)

Mud Pie

Mealtime Prayer:

Thank You, Lord, for the food we eat, for our family and the friends we meet. Each is special and unique! Amen.

Appetizer:

Q: Can you name three types of dirt?

A: Sand, silt, and clay.

The main difference between them is their size. "If a particle of sand were the size of a basketball, then silt would be the size of a baseball, and clay would be the size of a golf ball!"[1] What would your yard look like if dirt were really that size?

Main Course:

Is there a special place where you can dig in the mud? What do you like to make out of mud?

Q: When did God play in the mud?

A: When He formed Adam out of dirt! Read Genesis 2:7.

Table Talk:

- Why do you think God "formed" Adam instead of simply speaking him into existence like the other creatures?
- If you formed all the food on your plate into the shape of a man, could you make him come alive? Why or why not?
- How did God's "breath of life" make man different from the animals?
- What do you think God enjoyed most about forming you?

Vitamins and Minerals:

The LORD God formed the man . . . and breathed into his nostrils the breath of life, and the man became a living being. (Genesis 2:7)

---

1. "Facts of the Case: Soil Types," *The Great Plant Escape,* Urban Programs Resource Network, University of Illinois Extension Teacher's Guide, accessed June 3, 2013, http://urbanext.illinois.edu/gpe/case2/c2facts2.html.

Bible Trivia, Bonus Round

Mealtime Prayer:
The way God designed things (including the Bible) shows that He enjoys variety. Add new words to your mealtime prayer. For example: How would you describe your favorite hobby? Interesting? Fun? Action-packed? Can you apply any of these to God's blessings?

Appetizer:
Did you know that the Bible was written over a period of about 1,500 years? If you lived for 1,500 years, what hobbies would you take up?

Main Course:
Turn your meal into a *Jeopardy!* challenge round. Appoint one person to be the game host. Use these statements as game starters; then think of some of your own. (The answer needs to be given as a question!)

Q: There are 39 of them in the Old Testament and 27 in the New Testament.
A: What are the books of the Bible?
Q: The Gospels were named after these four men.
A: Who are Matthew, Mark, Luke, and John?
Q: This is a book of songs and praises.
A: What is the book of Psalms?

Table Talk:
- What are five things you can tell others about your favorite hobby?
- What are five things you can tell others about the Bible?
- Why is it important to know Bible facts?

Vitamins and Minerals:
For the word of God is living and active. (Hebrews 4:12)

That's Impossible!

Mealtime Prayer:

Pray this verse: "O LORD, you are my God; I will exalt you and praise your name, for in perfect faithfulness you have done marvelous things" (Isaiah 25:1).

Appetizer:

Q: How many pounds of fish or water can a pelican hold in its bill pouch?

A: Up to 27 pounds![1] Does this seem impossible? Check out the next question . . .

Q: How many colors can the human eye distinguish?

A: As many as 10 million distinct color variations.[2]

Main Course:

True or false? Answer these questions:

- God made a stick blossom and produce almonds (Numbers 17:1–8).
- God used bones to bring a dead man to life (2 Kings 13:21).
- God used a donkey to deliver a warning (Numbers 22:27–30).

Answer: They're all true! What other things has God used to do His work?

Table Talk:

- What does it mean for your life that God can do anything? How does it make you feel?
- Try to think of something God hasn't done yet. Then imagine ways He could do it.

Vitamins and Minerals:

Jesus looked at [the disciples] and said, "With man this is impossible, but with God all things are possible." (Matthew 19:26)

---

1. *National Geographic,* "Pelican: Pelecanus," accessed July 24, 2013, http://animals.nationalgeographic.com/animals/birds/pelican/
2. Deane B. Judd and Güther Wyszecki, *Color in Business, Science, and Industry, 3rd ed., Pure and Applied Optics* (New York: Wiley-Interscience, 1952), 295.

Grab the Biggest Peace

Mealtime Prayer:
Everybody should think of a person who is upset or lonely, or of a situation where people are angry at each other. Then get everyone to say a sentence prayer asking God to bring peace to that situation.

Appetizer:
Thankfully, we live in a relatively peaceful country. But there are still conflicts and disputes occurring. People go on strike or fight. People hurt each other. Can you name three groups of people who are on strike or fighting right now? Why are these disagreements or fights happening?

Main Course:
What do you think of when you hear the word *peacemaker*? One image might be of a mediator who is brought in to help striking employees come to an agreement with the company they are striking against. What other types of peacemakers can you think of? Who do you think Jesus was talking about when He said, "Blessed are the peacemakers" (Matthew 5:9)?

Table Talk:
- What is peace? What does it look like? Where does it come from?
- What's the difference between the way the world makes peace and the peace that God brings?
- When you are angry, sad, lonely, or upset, how can you find peace?
- Name five ways you can be a peacemaker at home, at school, or at work.

Vitamins and Minerals:
[Jesus said,] "Blessed are the peacemakers, for they will be called sons of God." (Matthew 5:9)

Freshly Squeezed

Mealtime Prayer:
Do a "squeeze prayer." Holding hands, have each person thank God for His love; then gently squeeze the next person's hand when finished.

Appetizer:
Did you know that freshly squeezed orange juice can last up to 168 hours in your refrigerator if stored in an airtight container? Think of five other fruits that can be squeezed for their juice.

Main Course:
Hugs are human squeezes. Did you know Jesus hugged children? Parents brought their little children to Jesus, and He took them into His arms and blessed them. You can read about it in Mark 10:13–16. How do you think Jesus' special attention made those children feel?

Table Talk:
- Close your eyes and imagine Jesus hugging you. What would it feel like? What would you tell Him? What do you think He would say to you?
- Why do you think Jesus said we must receive the kingdom of heaven like a child? How do children receive gifts?
- Why was Jesus angry with His disciples? What might they have learned when they saw Jesus with the children? What have you learned about the way Jesus loves each of us?

Vitamins and Minerals:
Jesus said, "Let the little children come to me, and do not hinder them, for the kingdom of heaven belongs to such as these." (Matthew 19:14)

Soup's Up!

Mealtime Prayer:

Thank God for things in alphabetical order. The first person thanks God for something that begins with an *A*, the next person a *B*, and so on until you thank God for 26 things, all the way through *Z*.

Appetizer:

Did you know that Americans eat more than 10 billion bowls of soup every year?[1] The first archaeological evidence of someone stirring up soup dates to between 5,000 and 9,000 BC.[2] The main ingredient for making broth is often bones from chicken, turkey, lamb, or cow. Think up other soup ingredients.

Main Course:

Has a family member ever made a bowl of soup for you when you were sick? How does soup make you feel better?

God likes to take care of you too. Luke 12:6–7 says, "Are not five sparrows sold for two pennies? Yet not one of them is forgotten by God. . . . Don't be afraid; you are worth more than many sparrows."

Table Talk:

- God feeds, clothes, and protects you. Does knowing this warm you up inside? In what other ways does God meet your needs?
- The Bible says that God knows the number of hairs on your head. What other interesting things does God know about you?

Vitamins and Minerals:

The LORD is good, a refuge in times of trouble. He cares for those who trust in him. (Nahum 1:7)

---

1. "About Us," Campbell's, accessed June 3, 2013, http://www.campbellsoup.com/Resources/AboutUs.
2. Research cited in Sarah Zielinski, "Stone Age Stew; Soup Making May Be Older Than We'd Thought," *The Salt* (blog), February 6, 2013, http://www.npr.org/blogs/thesalt/2013/02/06/171104410/stone-age-stew-soup-making-may-be-older-than-wed-thought.

Ba-Manna Splits

Mealtime Prayer:

Come, Lord Jesus, be our Guest. May this food by You be blessed. May our souls by You be fed. Ever on the Living Bread.

Appetizer:

Did you know that manna could be baked, boiled, ground, beaten, cooked in pans, and made into cakes? Do you think the Israelites ever made ba-manna splits? What about ba-manna cream pie? What other things could they have made?

Main Course:

Throughout the Old Testament, God used word pictures to represent Jesus Christ. Read Exodus 16. What did God provide for the Israelites who were wandering in the desert? How did it help them?

In the New Testament, Jesus referred to Himself as *true bread* or *true manna* (see John 6:32). Why? Jesus gives us life and satisfies our spiritual hunger. But His care lasts longer than 40 years. How long?

Table Talk:

- Manna fed the Israelites for 40 years. Why did manna show God's people His care?
- What other symbols in the Old Testament did God use to represent Jesus? What do they tell you about God?
- What is your favorite food? How many days could you eat it for breakfast, lunch, and dinner?

Vitamins and Minerals:

[Jesus said,] "It is my Father who gives you the true bread from heaven. For the bread of God is he who comes down from heaven and gives life to the world." (John 6:32–33)

Two's Company

Mealtime Prayer:
Thank God for your friends and family with whom you can share your many blessings. Thank Him also that He is your Father and that you can have a personal relationship with Him.

Appetizer:
God created you so that you would enjoy being with others. Take turns naming things that you enjoy doing with others, and why.

Can you enjoy being with someone even though you're not doing anything special? Why or why not?

Main Course:
Have you ever felt lonely? What is a sure cure for loneliness?

When there is no one else around, are you really alone? Why or why not? Who is with you? How do you know?

Table Talk:
- What is the best thing about having God always with you?
- If God is your friend, how can you be friends to Him?
- What can you do for someone you know who is lonely?
- What can you do if you are lonely?

Vitamins and Minerals:
We proclaim to you what we have seen and heard, so that you also may have fellowship with us. And our fellowship is with the Father and with his Son, Jesus Christ. (1 John 1:3)

Hide-and-Seek

Mealtime Prayer:
Thank God that He is always with us, that He watches over us, and that He always knows where we are.

Appetizer:

    Q: What game do mice like to play?
    A: Hide-and-squeak.

Main Course:

Let's play a quick game of hide-and-seek. Have one person hide. Everyone else must try to find the person who is hiding. Come back to the table when the person is found.

    How long did it take to find the one who was hiding? Why couldn't the others see the person who was hiding until they searched for a while? What special abilities would we need in order to see someone at all times? How can God see us no matter where we are? How can God see everyone at the same time?

Table Talk:

- If you could be in two places at the same time, where would you be?
- Does knowing that God can always see you make a difference in how you live? Give some examples.

Vitamins and Minerals:
Nothing in all creation is hidden from God's sight. (Hebrews 4:13)

Just a Drop in the Bucket?

Mealtime Prayer:

> *Dear Lord, thank You for loving us. Please help us to obey You in big things and in little things.*

Appetizer:

If you won a tanker truck full of your favorite drink in a bottle-cap-collecting contest, what beverage would you choose? Apart from drinking it, what are five things you could do with all that liquid?

Main Course:

Fill a clear glass pitcher or jar with water; then get some food coloring and have each family member add a drop or two to the water as you pass the pitcher around the table. What happens after you add one drop of food coloring? How about ten drops? Why?

Table Talk:

- Imagine that you are the jug of water and the food coloring is sin. What does sin do to you?
- What is sin? Name seven sins. Why is sin bad?
- What happens if you sin just once? What happens if you keep repeating the same sin?
- What has God done to help us break free from sin?
- What should you do if you sin?

Vitamins and Minerals:

Do not let sin reign in your mortal body so that you obey its evil desires. (Romans 6:12)

Cold Feet

Mealtime Prayer:

Think of times when God has helped you to have courage. Thank God for the courage He gives you.

Appetizer:

Have someone get a bucket of ice-cold water while everyone else takes off his or her socks and shoes. Now have each person take turns putting his or her feet in the bucket of water. How does it feel to have cold feet? What is another meaning for "cold feet"?

Main Course:

The Bible tells the story of a man named Peter who got cold feet one night—both kinds! He saw Jesus walking on top of the water and decided to join him. As he walked out on the water toward Jesus, the cold waves were tossing around him, and the wind was blowing fiercely.

Imagine being in Peter's place. How would you have felt? What would you have done?

Peter became frightened and began to sink, but Jesus reached out His hand and caught Peter (Matthew 14:25–31).

Table Talk:

- When do you get "cold feet"?
- How can Jesus help you when you are afraid?
- How can you help others who get cold feet?

Vitamins and Minerals:

[The Holy One says,] "So do not fear, for I am with you; do not be dismayed, for I am your God. I will strengthen you and help you; I will uphold you with my righteous right hand." (Isaiah 41:10)

Chicken Nuggets

Mealtime Prayer:

For food in a world where many walk in hunger,
For faith in a world where many walk in fear,
For friends in a world where many walk alone,
We give You humble thanks, O Lord. Amen.

Appetizer:

Q: Why don't chickens play baseball?
A: Because they hit fowl balls.

Main Course:

Have you ever had someone call you a chicken? Can you think of a person who's never been afraid? God knew that each of us would face times of fear. That's why He gave us "nuggets of truth."

Q: Guess how many times the Bible says, "Do not be afraid." Is it 10, 50, or 70 times?

A: Seventy

What things does the world tell you to worry about? Read Isaiah 43:5 and Luke 2:10. What do these verses tell you? With promises like that, you can give worries to God and leave chicken for the barbecue!

Table Talk:

- How does knowing God is with you help? Why?
- Was there a time this past week when you were afraid? What did you do?
- Name one worry you can give to God right now.

Vitamins and Minerals:

[Jesus said,] "Peace I leave with you; my peace I give you. I do not give to you as the world gives. Do not let your hearts be troubled and do not be afraid." (John 14:27)

Complete Confusion

Mealtime Prayer:
When you pray, ask God to help you be willing to learn from others in everything you do.

Appetizer:
Did you know that *dice* means to cut in cubes, and *whip* is to beat into a froth? What are some other cooking words you know?

Main Course:
Have you ever needed help reading a recipe? Words like *dice* and *whip* can be confusing. Sometimes the Bible can be confusing too!

Read Acts 8:30–31. Why didn't the Ethiopian understand God's Word? After Philip explained the passage, what did the man do? Why is it important that we help each other understand God's Word?

Table Talk:
- What could have happened if the Ethiopian had said, "Forget it; it's too hard"?
- What might have happened if Philip had said, "I can't help"?
- Who helps you understand God's Word?
- Who can you help understand God's Word? How?

Vitamins and Minerals:
You yourselves are full of goodness, complete in knowledge and competent to instruct one another. (Romans 15:14)

Garbageman to the Rescue!

Mealtime Prayer:
Have someone read the following prayer:
God, our Father, we thank You in prayer,
For forgiveness, for family, for food that we share. Amen.

Appetizer:
Did you know that the average person generates 4.4 pounds of waste each day? That's like throwing out 10 full boxes of macaroni and cheese.[1] What are the most common things your family throws away?

Main Course:
Did you know that God makes a good garbageman? What types of things does He like to remove from your heart and mind (jealousy, anger, etc.)? What does God do when you ask Him to help remove the garbage? How do you feel afterward? Thankfully, God's sin-disposal service comes more than once a week. In fact, it's available any time you ask!

Table Talk:
- What are some words you can use to describe garbage?
- What types of garbage tend to collect in your heart?
- What would you like God to remove right now? Ask Him to do so.

Vitamins and Minerals:
If we confess our sins, he is faithful and just and will forgive us our sins and purify us from all unrighteousness. (1 John 1:9)

---

1. Solid Waste District, LaPorte County, Indiana, "Garbage Statistics and Studies," accessed June 3, 2013, http://www.solidwastedistrict.com/information/stats.htm.

Jumbo Shrimp

Mealtime Prayer:

Lord, thank You that a shrimp like me is jumbo in Your eyes! Amen.

Appetizer:

Did you know that people in the United States ate almost twice as much shrimp as canned tuna in 2011?[1] What is your favorite seafood? Why?

Main Course:

Read Luke 19:1–10. Zacchaeus was a "shrimp." He was of small stature. What did he have to do to see Jesus? What does this tell you about Zacchaeus's heart? How did Jesus reward him?

Table Talk:

- Do you have a friend who is seeking God? How do you know he or she is seeking God? What can you say about Jesus to show your friend that Jesus is what he or she is looking for?
- Your friend may not be climbing trees looking for Jesus, but he or she might be asking questions about Jesus, church, or the Bible. What example does Jesus give about dealing with people who are seeking? Remember that every seeker of truth is "jumbo" (a big fish) in God's eyes!

Vitamins and Minerals:

Anyone who comes to [God] must believe that he exists and that he rewards those who earnestly seek him. (Hebrews 11:6)

---

1. National Marine Fisheries Service, "Top 10 Consumed Seafoods," accessed June 6, 2013, http://www.aboutseafood.com/about/about-seafood/top-10-consumed-seafoods.

Seven Spiritual Food Groups?

Mealtime Prayer:
Work together to come up with seven reasons why it's good to read the Bible. Then thank God for the wonderful gift of His Word.

Appetizer:
If you could eat one type of food, such as meat or vegetables, for the rest of your life, what would it be? Do you think you would ever get sick of it? What do you think would happen to your body if you ate only one type of food for five years?

Main Course:
After the food has been served, look at your plate. How many types of food do you see? Separate them into groups, such as meat, beans, grains, vegetables, and fruit. What's unique about each type? How do you tell the difference between a vegetable and a fruit? Between a nut and a grain? What does the food from one group give us that food from the other groups don't?

Table Talk:
Just as regular food comes in different types, so does "spiritual food." There are seven "spiritual food groups," or types of writings, in the Bible.
    Q: How many writing types in the Bible can you name?
    A: History, law, prophecy, poetry, wisdom, gospel, letter
- Why do you think the Bible contains so many different books?
- How are the types of Bible books like different food groups?
- What do we get from each type of writing that we don't get from the rest? What do we get from each type that is the same?

Vitamins and Minerals:
[Jesus said,] "It is written: 'Man does not live on bread alone, but on every word that comes from the mouth of God.' " (Matthew 4:4)

Chicken or Egg?

Mealtime Prayer:

Lord, we are truly grateful for the food before us. Thank You for the . . . [take turns thanking God for the foods on your table]. Amen.

Appetizer:

How do you think the first Life Savers candy was invented? The machine that Clarence A. Crane was using to "produce a new kind of mint candy malfunctioned and . . . punched a hole in the center."[1] It was an accidental invention that became the first Life Saver.

What firsts did you have this past year?

Main Course:

Are you a first-rate Bible scholar? Answer these firsts:

Q: What was Christ's first miracle?
A: Turning water into wine (John 2:3–11).
Q: When was the first time God told someone to store food?
A: When Noah was packing the ark (Genesis 6:21).
Q: What came first, the chicken or the egg?
A: The chicken (Genesis 1:20–21).

Table Talk:

- Why would God record all these firsts?
- The Bible passages mentioned above are about God's care for people. What do they tell you about God?
- How else does God provide?

Vitamins and Minerals:

[God] makes grass grow for the cattle, and plants for man to cultivate—bringing forth food from the earth. (Psalm 104:14)

---

1. Sandra and Harry Choron, *The All-New Book of Lists for Kids* (New York: Houghton Mifflin, 2002), 190.

Feeling Sheepish?

Mealtime Prayer:

Thank God for being your Shepherd and wanting you in His flock.

Appetizer:

Q: Are there are more sheep or people in Australia?

A: There are slightly more than seven sheep for every person.[1]

What would your house be like if there were more pets than people in it?

Main Course:

The Bible often refers to God as our Shepherd. Name things that a shepherd does. How is God like a shepherd? How is being a shepherd like being a pet owner? How are you like sheep?

Table Talk:

- If God is the "pet owner" and you're the "pet," how does He treat you? Why?
- How do you feel knowing God's looking out for you?
- How are you different from a pet? How does God treat you differently than a pet owner would treat you? Why?

Vitamins and Minerals:

[God] tends his flock like a shepherd: He gathers the lambs in his arms and carries them close to his heart. (Isaiah 40:11)

---

1. Statistics New Zealand, "Population Mythbusters: New Zealand Is Home to 3 Million People and 60 Million Sheep," June 22, 2012, http://www.stats.govt.nz/browse_for_stats/population/myth busters/3million-people-60million-sheep.aspx.

Spread the Mustard

Mealtime Prayer:

As you thank God for your blessings, ask Him to give you faith to believe in His Word and to trust Him in all things.

Appetizer:

If you have a jar of mustard seed in your spice cabinet, place a few seeds on a plate and set them on the table. (If you don't have seeds, pick a few out of a jar of stone-ground mustard.) How big is a mustard seed? Compare it to other items. Did you know that the oil from mustard seeds is used for making soap? What are some other possible uses for mustard seeds? Be creative.

Main Course:

The Bible says that if we have faith the size of a mustard seed (that's not very much!), nothing will be impossible for us (Matthew 17:20). If by believing you could make something true, what would you believe? Why?

Table Talk:

- Where does faith come from?
- What things are true whether you believe them or not? How do you know?
- What can you believe in that is absolutely true and reliable?
- How can faith give you peace and confidence?

Vitamins and Minerals:

[Jesus said,] "If you have faith as small as a mustard seed, you can say to this mountain, 'Move from here to there,' and it will move. Nothing will be impossible for you." (Matthew 17:20)

Scrambled or Fried?

Mealtime Prayer:
Thank God that He has a plan and purpose for your life. Ask Him to use you according to His will.

Appetizer:
Place a carton of eggs on the table. Talk about the different ways that eggs can be used. How do you like your eggs prepared? If you were an egg, how would you like to be used?

Main Course:
Eggs look very similar, but they can be used for many different purposes: for breakfast, in baked goods, to make stiff meringue on a pie. How are Christians like eggs? How does God use Christians in different ways? If God can do anything, why does He use Christians? What would happen if all Christians were used in the same way?

Table Talk:
- How do you think God decides who He is going to use and how He will use them?
- What do we need to do in order for God to use us?
- What special job do you think God has planned for you?

Vitamins and Minerals:
There are different kinds of gifts, but the same Spirit. There are different kinds of service, but the same Lord. (1 Corinthians 12:4–5)

Inside and Out

Mealtime Prayer:
Thank God for the food, and ask Him to help your family to be honest and sincere in all you do.

Appetizer:
If you were going to write a book about your life, what would you call it? What would the cover look like? Who would read it?

Main Course:
Before the meal, find two hardcover books that are exactly the same size. Secretly exchange the jackets; then bring one of them to the table. Let everyone look at it—but don't let them open it. Then ask: Judging by the book's cover, what do you think it is about? How do you know? Would you like to read the book? Why or why not?

Now have someone open the book to the title page and read it out loud. Would you like to read the book now? Why or why not?

Table Talk:
- Have you ever met people who appeared to be something they were not? How did you feel about them?
- What is it like to meet someone who is exactly who he or she appears to be? Why?
- Which kind of person would you rather be? Why?

Vitamins and Minerals:
Even a child is known by his actions, by whether his conduct is pure and right. (Proverbs 20:11)

Quiet, Please!

Mealtime Prayer:

Ask God to help you live peacefully with one another and to be kind and thoughtful to each other. Thank Him for your family and for the blessings He has given you.

Appetizer:

Have one person take a sheet of paper and draw a line down the center. On one side of the paper, write down some harsh words people use. On the other side, write some gentle words they give you. What kinds of feelings go with saying and hearing the harsh words? What about the gentle words?

Main Course:

Why do people use harsh words? How do you feel when someone uses them with you? What is a gentle answer? How can a gentle answer help settle an argument? How do you feel when someone uses gentle words with you?

Table Talk:

- What should you do if you get into an argument?
- How can you disagree with someone without arguing?
- How can you be a peacemaker?
- Why would God want His followers to be peacemakers?

Vitamins and Minerals:

A gentle answer turns away wrath, but a harsh word stirs up anger. (Proverbs 15:1)

The Big Apple

Mealtime Prayer:

Along with thanking God for your food, also thank Him for the people who shared a "seed of faith" with the members of your family (people who told each of you about Jesus).

Appetizer:

Did you know that apples are members of the rose family?[1]

Q: What did Johnny Appleseed share at the same time he was sharing his apple seeds?

A: The good news about Jesus.

Main Course:

Did you know that the apples from one tree can fill 20 boxes every year?[2] Consider this old saying: "You can count the seeds in one apple, but you can't count the apples in one seed." Think about it. What does this mean?

When you tell your friends about Jesus, you share seeds of faith with them (1 Corinthians 9:11). What can happen with these seeds? How are your friends like "the apples in one seed"?

Table Talk:

- When you tell someone about Jesus, how many lives could you be affecting? Will you ever know? When?
- What's one very cool thing you can share about Jesus?
- What do you like best about apples?

Vitamins and Minerals:

[Jesus said,] "Other seed fell on good soil, where it produced a crop—a hundred, sixty or thirty times what was sown." (Matthew 13:8)

---

1. University of Illinois Extension, "Apples and More: Apple Facts," accessed June 3, 2013, http://urbanext.illinois.edu/apples/facts.cfm.

2. Ibid.

All Ears!

Mealtime Prayer:
Many families hold hands during mealtime prayer and close their eyes to concentrate on God. Do this today, and listen carefully to the one praying.

Appetizer:
Q: What has ears but can't hear?
A: A cornfield.
Popcorn pops because it has water inside the kernels. When it is heated, the pressure of the steam builds; then the kernel finally explodes.[1]

Main Course:
Play a game before dessert that will help you use your ears.
1. Blindfold a child, and choose one parent for the child to find.
2. Place the blindfolded person in the center of the room. Everyone else moves to the corners.
3. Everyone calls out directions to his or her corner. The blindfolded person must follow only the voice of the chosen parent.
4. Finding the correct corner means the child wins!

Table Talk:
- Every day we hear many "voices." What advice do you get from the "voices" of movies, music, friends? Whose voice should you follow?
- What types of advice do your parents give? What happens when you concentrate on their words and obey them?
- What is one command that's difficult to obey? Why?

Vitamins and Minerals:
Listen, my son, to your father's instruction and do not forsake your mother's teaching. (Proverbs 1:8)

---

1. NASA for Kids, "What Makes Popcorn Pop?" August 5, 2003, http://www.nasa.gov/audience /forkids/home/popcorn.html.

It's All Gravity

Mealtime Prayer:

Ask every person at the table to think of someone in their life who has helped them know God better in some way. (A pastor, relative, neighbor, or friend.) Say a prayer of thanks for those people.

Appetizer:

Match the correct answer below to each question.

A. weight B. gravity C. lower

1. What is the force that keeps the moon revolving around the earth?
2. Your _____ is the force of the Earth's gravity pulling you down onto its surface.
3. The force of gravity is _____ on the moon than on Earth.

(Answers: 1–B, 2–A, 3–C)

Main Course:

Gravity is described as the pulling force that exists between things. How can people be like a pulling force when it comes to affecting the way we think? How can this force pull us toward God or away from God?

Table Talk:

- Name a time when you felt someone was pulling you away from God.
- Now name a time when you felt someone pull you closer to God.
- What are ways we can pull people away from God? How can we pull them toward Him?

Vitamins and Minerals:

Therefore encourage one another and build each other up, just as in fact you are doing. (1 Thessalonians 5:11)

Rubbing Shoulders

Mealtime Prayer:

Lord God almighty, bless us here today. May we grow in strength and wisdom as we spend time with You. Amen.

Appetizer:

If you could buy any three toys or games, what would they be? Why? Where did you hear about these items? How does watching commercials affect you? How do things we see and hear change how we feel? How do people we hang out with change us?

Main Course:

Read Acts 4:3–13. After Jesus returned to heaven, what happened to Peter and John? How did they change after being with Jesus? What changed them? Why? They didn't even stop telling people about Jesus when they were put in jail. How did the priest know they had been with Jesus?

Table Talk:

- How can your parents tell who or what you've been spending a lot of time with?
- How will others know you've been with Jesus?
- Name three reasons why Jesus is a good influence.

Vitamins and Minerals:

When [the religious leaders] saw the courage of Peter and John and realized that they were unschooled, ordinary men, they were astonished and they took note that these men had been with Jesus. (Acts 4:13)

Miles in His Shoes

Mealtime Prayer:

Help us, dear Jesus, every day
To follow You in every way;
To glorify and honor You
In everything we say and do. Amen.

Appetizer:

How long would it take for you to walk from one end of your town to the other? What would you take with you?

Main Course:

When Jesus lived on earth, He walked from town to town teaching people about God and healing people who were sick. One day Jesus asked 12 of His friends to help Him. The 12 men who agreed to follow Jesus were called His disciples.

What do you think it would have been like to be with Jesus all day? What would be hard about being a disciple? What did they have to leave behind? What do you think the disciples brought with them?

Table Talk:

- If Jesus lived here today, where would you follow Him and how could you help Him?
- What would you leave behind? What would you gain?
- Jesus is here right now. How can you follow Him in your life?

Vitamins and Minerals:

Jesus said to his disciples, "If anyone would come after me, he must deny himself and take up his cross and follow me." (Matthew 16:24)

Goin' Down!

Mealtime Prayer:

As you thank God for His blessings, thank Him for the gift of faith and the opportunity to bring others to Him.

Appetizer:

If you had to cut a hole in your roof, what tools would you need? How long do you think it would take? Why would it be dangerous? What possible reason could make you do it?

Main Course:

The Bible tells the story of some men who had a great reason to bring down the roof. They wanted to take their sick friend to Jesus. They knew that Jesus could make their friend better, but they couldn't get near Him because it was too crowded. Read what happened in Mark 2:2–5, 11–12.

Table Talk:

- How long do you think it took to cut through the roof?
- How is Jesus' response different from what your parents' would be if you cut a hole in the roof? Why?
- How hard would you work to bring your friends to Jesus?

Vitamins and Minerals:

Now faith is being sure of what we hope for and certain of what we do not see. (Hebrews 11:1)

Frogs for Dinner

Mealtime Prayer:
Think about how big and powerful God is. Then praise Him for times when He has made His way clear to you.

Appetizer:
Write the Egyptian plagues (water turned to blood, boils, frogs, hail, lice, death of cattle, locust, flies, darkness, and death of firstborn) on pieces of paper, and put them into a bowl. Take turns choosing a paper and then drawing a picture of the plague until someone guesses it.

Main Course:
How would you try to convince someone to do what you wanted? The people of Israel were slaves in Egypt. Moses asked Pharaoh to let them leave, but Pharaoh said no. Why would Pharaoh do that?

God had a unique way to convince Pharaoh to change his mind. God sent plagues. After the firstborn in every Egyptian family died, Pharaoh told Moses to get out of town!

Table Talk:
- What might have happened if Pharaoh had let the people leave after the first plague?
- Why do you think Pharaoh was so stubborn? What can happen when people think they are greater than God?
- What was God showing Pharaoh, Egypt, and His people about himself?
- How would you like God to convince you to do things His way?

Vitamins and Minerals:
Yours, O LORD, is the greatness and the power and the glory and the majesty and the splendor, for everything in heaven and earth is yours. Yours, O LORD, is the kingdom; you are exalted as head over all. (1 Chronicles 29:11)

Just Say "Cheese"

Mealtime Prayer:
Think of some things that make you happy. Thank God for those things.

Appetizer:

Q: If Swiss cheese comes from Switzerland, where does cottage cheese come from?

A: Someone's cottage. Middle European housewives made it at home.[1]

How many different kinds of cheese can you name? What is your favorite? What do you do with cheese?

Main Course:
Have everyone say "cheese" and smile a big cheesy smile. How do you feel when you smile? Why is smiling good for us? Why are our smiles good for others?

Think of 10 reasons why you can be happy. How does being happy affect our relationships with others?

Table Talk:
- Do you think God wants us to be happy? Why or why not?
- Often just thinking of what God has done for us makes us happy. What has God done for you that makes you feel happy?
- How can we help others to be happy?

Vitamins and Minerals:
A cheerful heart is good medicine, but a crushed spirit dries up the bones. (Proverbs 17:22)

---

1. Wisconsin Milk Marketing Board, "Cottage Cheese," accessed June 4, 2013, http://eat wisconsin-cheese.com/cheese/article.aspx?cid=76.

Peanut Problems?

Mealtime Prayer:
Praise God for His righteousness (moral goodness). Ask Him to help you live in a way that is pleasing to Him.

Appetizer:
Are you allergic to any kind of food? You probably know someone either in your family or at your school who is allergic to peanuts. About two kids in a hundred can't tolerate this food. Some kids are so allergic, they could die from exposure to this nut.[1]

Doctors also don't know of any cure for peanut allergies. The best thing to do if you're allergic is to stay far away from them.

Main Course:
The Bible tells us that God can't tolerate certain things either. What are some sins that God hates? What happens when you do those things? There are some things that God loves, too.

What does righteousness mean? (Right living.) Why do you think God loves righteousness? What are some other things that God loves? What happens when you do those things consistently?

Table Talk:
- Sin leads to unhappiness in the long run, if not right away. So, why do people sin?
- Why do you think God wants us to be righteous? (For example, He knows it will make us do good.)
- How do you think God feels when we obey Him? When we disobey?

Vitamins and Minerals:
Just as he who called you is holy, so be holy in all you do. (1 Peter 1:15)

---

1. Charlotte Libov, "Fascinating Facts About Peanut Allergies," EverydayHealth.com, last modified December 21, 2012, accessed June 5, 2013, http://www.everydayhealth.com/allergy-pictures /fascinating-facts-about-peanut-allergies.aspx#/slide-1.

Eggs-actly Like Jesus!

Mealtime Prayer:

Sing this prayer to the tune of "London Bridge":

God is great and God is good, God is good, God is good.
Let us thank Him for this food. Alleluia!

Appetizer:

Q: How long does it take a hen to produce an egg?

A: Twenty-four to seventy-two hours, depending on the breed and age of the chicken.[1]

Q: What kind of hens produce white-shelled eggs? Brown-shelled eggs?

A: White-shelled eggs are produced by hens with white ear lobes, and brown-shelled eggs are produced by hens with red ear lobes. Really.[2]

Main Course:

Play an eggs-citing game of charades: Write the names of family members on separate pieces of paper. Put the names into a bowl. Add a few slips with "Jesus" on them and another few with "hen" on them. Each family member takes a turn drawing a name to role-play. The person who guesses the answer gets to go next. Pay special attention to how people portray Jesus. Give everyone a high five for doing an egg-cellent job!

Table Talk:

- How do we behave when we're acting like Jesus?
- Is it possible to mimic His actions throughout the day? How?
- Why should you copy Jesus?

Vitamins and Minerals:

[Jesus said,] "Whoever serves me must follow me." (John 12:26)

---

1. Murray McMurray Hatchery, "Frequently Asked Questions," accessed June 3, 2013, http://www.mcmurrayhatchery.com/faqhowlongdoesi.html.

2. BackYard Chickens, "Chicken FAQ's—The Frequent Asked Questions of Raising Chickens," last modified March 19, 2012, http://www.backyardchickens.com/a/chicken-faqs-the-frequent-asked-questions-of-raising-chickens.

No Mis-steaks!

Mealtime Prayer:

Thank the Lord that He is perfect and for the wonderful things He has made, such as the Bible, good food, and your family!

Appetizer:

Q: People in what country consume more steak than anyone else?

A: Argentina—each person eats 140 pounds of beef on average each year.[1]

Q: How many people wrote the Bible?

A: More than 30.

Q: What was the first book to be printed on a printing press?

A: The Bible in around 1455.[2]

Main Course:

There are many "mis-steaks" when it comes to the world of food. Have you ever heard of a London broil steak? Surprisingly, London broil is actually the name of a recipe, not a cut of beef. Butchers still mislabel several different beef cuts "London broil." While there are "mis-steaks" all around us, where is one place there are no mistakes? That's right, the Bible!

Table Talk:

- The Bible is a complete story from beginning to end. How do you think God accomplished this? What could that one story be?
- Why does it matter to you that God kept His Word free of mistakes?

Vitamins and Minerals:

All Scripture is God-breathed and is useful for teaching, rebuking, correcting and training in righteousness, so that the man of God may be thoroughly equipped for every good work. (2 Timothy 3:16–17)

---

1. Purdue University: Food Animal Education Network, "Beef Facts," last modified November 29, 2009, accessed June 3, 2013, http://www.ansc.purdue.edu/faen/beef%20facts.html.
2. Harry Ransom Center: University of Texas at Austin, "The Gutenberg Bible," accessed June 3, 2013, http://www.hrc.utexas.edu/exhibitions/permanent/gutenbergbible/facts/#top/.

Icing on the Cake!

Mealtime Prayer:
(Tune: "Row, Row, Row Your Boat")
> *Thank You, thank You, thank You, Lord,*
> *For the food we eat.*
> *It's so very nice of You*
> *To make some of it sweet!*

Appetizer:
> Q: Why did the student eat her homework?
> A: The teacher told her it was a piece of cake.

Did you know that the tallest cake ever made was just over 108 feet and used over 7,000 pounds of eggs?[1] Would you be able to make a cake half that size in your kitchen?

Main Course:

Just as a good cake is made up of the finest ingredients, so God's character is made up of only the best. What are some of His "ingredients"? Here are a few to get you started: loving, generous, forgiving. Try to come up with a word to describe God for each letter in your name.

Table Talk:
- God is not cake, but how can you "taste and see that the LORD is good" (Psalm 34:8)?
- What are some ingredients that God gives you when you spend time with Him?

Vitamins and Minerals:
The LORD our God is righteous in everything he does. (Daniel 9:14)

---

1. "Tallest Cake," Guinness World Records, accessed June 3, 2013, http://www.guinnessworldrecords .com/world-records/1/tallest-cake-.

No Busy Signals

Mealtime Prayer:
On the count of three, have everybody say his or her own grace quietly.

Appetizer:
If you could talk to God on the phone tonight and ask Him just one question, what would it be? How do you think He would answer? If God left you a message on your answering machine, what would you like Him to say?

Main Course:
Have you ever tried to phone in to enter a contest on a radio station? What happened? Did you win? Most likely you got a busy signal instead. Why would that have happened? How did you feel?

Table Talk:
- How many prayers do you think God hears in an average day? Do you think He answers them all? Why or why not?
- How can you know God hears your prayers? Is there a time in the past month or year when you saw Him answer your prayers? If so, what happened?
- Does knowing that God hears your prayers make you want to pray more or less? Why?

Vitamins and Minerals:
This is the confidence we have in approaching God: that if we ask anything according to his will, he hears us. (1 John 5:14)

No Crying Over Spilled Milk

Mealtime Prayer:

Jesus told us to pray, "Give us today our daily bread. Forgive us our debts, as we also have forgiven our debtors" (Matthew 6:11–12). Give family members the chance to pray silently for their meal and ask for forgiveness.

Appetizer:

Fold a paper towel several times; then drop splotches of food coloring onto it. Open the paper towel. What picture do you see in your pattern?

Main Course:

In the early 1930s people everywhere started snatching up a new product: personal disposable tissue towels.[1] Overnight, life in the kitchen became easier. There was no more crying over spilled milk—it could be wiped up in just one swipe!

What other things are paper towels used for? But paper towels cannot clean up big messes like the sins in our hearts. Why not? What is the only way to remove the stain of sin?

Table Talk:

- Psalm 51:7 says, "Wash me, [LORD,] and I will be whiter than snow." How does God wash you?
- Give Jesus your "spilled milk" by confessing your sins. Then ask Him to forgive you and clean you up.

Vitamins and Minerals:

"Come now, let us reason together," says the LORD. "Though your sins are like scarlet, they shall be as white as snow." (Isaiah 1:18)

---

1. "One Teacher's Fight Against Germs: Disposable Paper Towels Story," Kimberly-Clark, http://www.cms.kimberly-clark.com/umbracoimages/UmbracoFileMedia/ProductEvol_PaperTowel_umbracoFile.pdf; originally published in Robert Spector, *Shared Values: A History of Kimberly-Clark* (Lyme: CT: Greenwich Publishing Group, 1997).

The Journey of a Lifetime

Mealtime Prayer:

The Bible gives us clear directions for prayer. In Matthew 6:9–11, Jesus told us to pray to "our Father in heaven," thanking Him for our "daily bread." Give each family member a chance to do this.

Appetizer:

Did you know that the Bible has more than 30,000 verses?[1] That's a lot of directions! If you have memorized any scriptures, say one now.

Main Course:

Have you ever kept track of your vacation trip on a map? It's exciting to see where you've been, where you are, and where you're going. Name two ways that the Bible is like a map for our lives. Next, read these verses, and answer the questions.

- Romans 3:23: Where are we before we accept Jesus' gift of grace? (Stuck in sin)
- Acts 10:43: Where are we after we repent? (Forgiven in Jesus)
- 1 Peter 1:4: Where are we going? (Heaven)

Table Talk:

- If your best friend lived far away, and you had to travel to his or her house, what five things would you take with you?
- Why can you be excited about the journey the Bible leads you on?
- What are some of the directions the Bible gives to help you on your journey through life?

Vitamins and Minerals:

Show me your ways, O Lord, teach me your paths. (Psalm 25:4)

---

1. "How many verses are there in the Bible?" Dear Digger Doug, Discoverymagazine.com, copyright © 2002 Apologetics Press, accessed June 5, 2013, http://www.discoverymagazine.com/digger/d02dd/d0203dd.html.

The Opposite Game

Mealtime Prayer:

Ask God to give you wisdom to make the right choices. Thank Him for the wisdom in His Word.

Appetizer:

Let's play the Opposite game. Think of an opposite word for the following words: *tall, black, hard, quiet, cold, happy, sour, true, rough, in, near, foolish.*

Main Course:

The book of Proverbs has many verses that show how *wise* is the opposite of *foolish*. If you were really wise, how could you change your world? What are some wise things that people do? What foolish things do people do? Why do they do foolish things? Who do you think is happier, a wise person or a foolish person? Why?

Table Talk:

- How can we become wise?
- What should we do if we can't decide whether something is wise or foolish?
- Name three things you need wisdom about. How can you get it?

Vitamins and Minerals:

Be very careful, then, how you live—not as unwise but as wise. (Ephesians 5:15)

In His Image

Mealtime Prayer:
Thank God for creating you in His image so that you can have a relationship with Him.

Appetizer:
Look at the people sitting around the table. Describe how you are alike and how you are different.

Main Course:
What are some of the things that God created? How were Adam and Eve different from the rest of creation? Imagine being in a garden of Eden that God made especially for you.

Table Talk:
- Why do you think God created people in His image? What does "in His image" mean?
- How are we like God? How are we different from God?
- Why do you think God made such a perfect place for Adam and Eve? To you, what would have been the best thing about the garden of Eden? (See Genesis 2:8–14.)

Vitamins and Minerals:
God created man in his own image, in the image of God he created him; male and female he created them. (Genesis 1:27)

Need Directions?

Mealtime Prayer:
Thank God for the directions He gives us. Ask Him to help you understand and follow them.

Appetizer:
Have someone give directions from (1) home to church; (2) your house to the nearest park or playground; (3) sadness to happiness.

Main Course:
Think of a time when you've been lost. How did you feel? How did you find your way? What happens if we follow the wrong directions? Why is it important to know where we are going? It's important to know where you're going in life, too. Why do we need directions for living?

Table Talk:
- Where can we find the right directions for living?
- Why can we trust God's directions?
- What are three of His directions (for example, don't lie)?

Vitamins and Minerals:
Trust in the LORD with all your heart and lean not on your own understanding; in all your ways acknowledge him, and he will make your paths straight. (Proverbs 3:5–6)

Solve the Mystery

Mealtime Prayer:
Ask God to help you understand the truth in the Bible.

Appetizer:
Go to your bookshelf and find a mystery book, but keep it hidden from those at the table. Flip it open and read a paragraph. Have people guess what the story is about. Why do some people like reading mysteries, while others don't? What is the best part of a mystery? What mysteries would you like answers to?

Main Course:
Some people think of the Bible as a mystery book because they don't understand what the writers are saying. The prophets often foretold events that were going to happen. There's a mystery! How did they know about the future? (See Hebrews 1:1.)

In the New Testament, the apostle Paul said that God has made known the mystery that has been hidden throughout the ages. What is it? (See Colossians 1:27.)

Table Talk:
- In some ways, the Bible is a book with many layers. How does Jesus help us understand it?
- It's also a book that answers other mysteries, like how to find true happiness. What other mysteries does the Bible explain?

Vitamins and Minerals:
Oh, the depth of the riches of the wisdom and knowledge of God! How unsearchable his judgments, and his paths beyond tracing out! (Romans 11:33)

Lean on Me!

Mealtime Prayer:
Pick out one of your favorite Christian songs and have everyone "hum" it together while thinking about the words.

Appetizer:
You need one sheet from a newspaper for this activity.

Q: How can two people stand on the same sheet of paper, face-to-face, so they can't possibly touch each other? No, the people's hands aren't tied. And you can't tear the sheet of paper or touch each other in any way. Try it.

A: Any doorway will do. Place the sheet of paper so half is on one side of the door and half is on the other, with the door closed in between.

Main Course:
How can a family be like this: standing on the same things but unable to reach or touch each other? Families sometimes go through hard times and difficult challenges. What are some difficult situations that a family might have to face? Talk about some of the hardest things your family has gone through. Why were they hard? How did you get through them?

Table Talk:
- Whom did you lean on during a hard time? Why did it help you to lean on that person?
- What made the "door open" between you?
- Who is always there and ready to help you get through difficult times?
- How can you lean on Him?

Vitamins and Minerals:
God is our refuge and strength, an ever-present help in trouble. (Psalm 46:1)

Tell Me a Story

Mealtime Prayer:

Thank You, Father, for Your Word,
For stories that we've often heard.
Help us learn Your truth today.
Hear us, Father, as we pray. Amen.

Appetizer:

What's your favorite fairy tale or fable? Who can tell the story about "The Little Red Hen" or "The Fox and the Crow"?

Main Course:

Q: If you have one ox and someone gives you another ox, what do you have?

A: Parables—pair of bulls.

Jesus was a fantastic storyteller. Many times when Jesus was teaching His disciples or large groups of people, He told interesting stories called parables (see Matthew 13). Why do you think He used stories?

Table Talk:

- The parables teach people how God wants them to live and treat one another. How many can you name or tell?
- Do you have a favorite parable? If so, what is it? What does it mean?
- Why are Jesus' parables recorded in the Bible?
- Choose a parable (one you know or one from Matthew 13, 18, or 21:28—22:14). How can it help you?

Vitamins and Minerals:

Let me understand the teaching of your precepts; then I will meditate on your wonders. (Psalm 119:27)

Seeds and Sprouts

Mealtime Prayer:
Thank God for the uniqueness of each person in your family.
Name at least one special talent or gift for each person that you
are thankful for.

Appetizer:
Most plants come from seeds. Name a few foods that still have
seeds when you eat them.
> Q: How many sesame seeds are there on a McDonald's Big Mac bun?
> A: About 178![1]

Main Course:
Each plant comes from a unique seed, and within the dry husk lies all the hidden facts about the future plant. What "facts" does a corn kernel know about a corn plant?

Just as a farmer chooses the seeds he wants, so God chose special characteristics and talents and placed them deep inside you. How are you like that corn kernel? Close your eyes for a moment and picture the seeds God chose for you.

Table Talk:
- What are the special talents God planted deep inside you? How do they tell you who you could be one day?
- What can you do to cultivate your special gifts?
- Name three ways sprouting these gifts can work at your church and at school.

Vitamins and Minerals:
[Jesus said,] "If you have faith as small as a mustard seed, you can say to this mountain, 'Move from here to there,' and it will move. Nothing will be impossible for you." (Matthew 17:20)

---

1. McPennsylvania/North Huntingdon, "Big Mac Facts and Trivia," accessed June 6, 2013, http://www.mcpennsylvania.com/3115/3812/Big-Mac-Facts/.

"Lettuce" Pray

Mealtime Prayer:

We thank You, Father, for our evening meal,
For fun and friends and the joy we feel.
For blessing and guidance and love we pray.
Be with us now and each new day. Amen.

Appetizer:

Did you know that lettuce is a member of the sunflower family? One kind of lettuce is called *crisphead*. But in the 1930s people began calling it *iceberg* lettuce when Fresh Express in California began transporting lettuce underneath mounds of ice to keep it cool.[1] Can you think of four other foods that need to be kept cold while they're being transported to stores?

Main Course:

Make your own "Lettuce Pray Salad." On green construction paper, have each person write his or her own prayer. Then write down different "ingredients" to add to your prayer salad. Thankfulness and confession are two possibilities. Toss these prayers in a bowl, and then lift the bowl heavenward as a symbol of your family offering prayers to God.

Table Talk:

- Why would God enjoy a "salad" like this?
- What else could you add to this type of salad?

Vitamins and Minerals:

Pray in the Spirit on all occasions with all kinds of prayers and requests. (Ephesians 6:18)

---

1. The Kitchen Project: Food History, "The History of Iceberg Lettuce," accessed June 6, 2013, http://kitchenproject.com/history/Salads_Lettuce/IceburgLettuce.htm.

Fresh-Baked "Roll" Models

Mealtime Prayer:
Jesus prayed that the world would know the love of God (John 17:23). Use His example for your prayer today. Pray that the world can see God's love through your family; then thank God for your meal.

Appetizer:
Did you know that the proper etiquette for eating rolls is to break them in half or in small pieces before buttering and eating them? What are two other table manners?

Main Course:
Has someone ever said to you, "I could tell right away that you were part of that family"? What might give you away? Why? Even if you don't look like anyone else in your family, perhaps you walk like your father or talk like your mother.

What is a role model? How are your parents your role models? What other people are role models in your life? How can you distinguish between good and bad role models?

Table Talk:
- What about you helps others recognize that you are part of God's family?
- Why was Jesus the perfect role model? Why did He tell His disciples to copy Him in all things?
- In what ways did Jesus show us how to love?

Vitamins and Minerals:
[Jesus said,] "A new command I give you: Love one another. As I have loved you, so you must love one another. By this all men will know that you are my disciples, if you love one another." (John 13:34–35)

Simon Says—God Says!

Mealtime Prayer:
God says that we should pray for each other (Ephesians 6:18).
Take time to do this after thanking God for your food.

Appetizer:
Did you know that because people obey God and tell others about
Jesus, the Bible or New Testament has been translated into over 1,793
languages?[1] If you could learn another language, which would you choose?

Main Course:
Play a game of Simon Says, giving everyone an opportunity to be Simon.

The Bible gives us instructions too. Think of it as God Says. God tells us
what we should do when we're sitting, walking, and lying down. It doesn't matter what we're doing, we should always think about what God says.

Table Talk:
- What was your favorite instruction in Simon Says? What was the most
  difficult to follow?
- What is your favorite Bible instruction? What is the most difficult to
  follow?
- What happens when you don't obey what God says? (Remember that
  God is faithful to forgive.) How can you check what you're doing with
  what God says?

Vitamins and Minerals:
Fix these words of mine in your hearts and minds. . . . [Talk] about them when
you sit at home and when you walk along the road, when you lie down and
when you get up. (Deuteronomy 11:18–19)

---

1. Wycliffe.org, "What's Been Done, What's Left to Do: Latest Bible Translation Statistics," last modified September 2012, accessed June 6, 2013, http://wycliffe.org.uk/wycliffe/about/vision-what
wedo.html.

Forecast: Heavenly Sunshine

Mealtime Prayer:

Dear Lord, shine Your love upon this table and on every heart present. Amen.

Appetizer:

On what kind of days do you feel your best, sunny days or cloudy days? Did you know that along with food and exercise, you need sunshine to make you healthy? Sun gives your body vitamin D. In fact, children who don't get enough vitamin D could get a disease called rickets.[1] How do you feel when you don't get enough sun?

Main Course:

What do you think Jesus looks like? Read Revelation 1:13–16 for a description of how the apostle John saw Jesus. How does this image of Jesus show His power and glory? How is your idea of Jesus different from the one John saw?

The Bible says, "The LORD God is a sun" (Psalm 84:11). How has He been your "sunshine" today?

Table Talk:

- What parts of God's character help you feel better?
- How are God and the sun similar? (Example: The sun warms our bodies; God warms our hearts with His love.)
- Which is greater, God's sun or God's Son? Why?
- How can the sun remind you of God's presence this week?

Vitamins and Minerals:

For the LORD God is a sun and shield. (Psalm 84:11)

---

1. Mayo Clinic Staff, "Rickets," Mayo Clinic, June 1, 2013, http://www.mayoclinic.com/health/rickets/DS00813.

Native American Thanks

Mealtime Prayer:

Eagles thank God for the mountains. (Flap arms like wings.)
Fish thank God for the sea. (Put hands together like a swimming fish.)
We thank God for our blessings, (Bow heads, fold hands.)
For what we're about to receive. (Open hands toward dinner table.)

Appetizer:

Pumpkins, zucchini, sweet potatoes, turkey, peanuts, and maple syrup are all of Native American origin. What foods are you most thankful for?

Texas comes from a Native American word that means *friend*. About half of the US state names are derived from Native American names.[1] Guess which ones. What do you appreciate most about the place where you live? How can you thank God for that?

Main Course:

Create a special centerpiece for your table. Have each family member choose one item to represent something he or she is thankful for. (For example, a clothespin can represent the clothing God provides for your family.) Each say a simple prayer of thanks as you place your items on the table.

Table Talk:

- Why is it important to say thank you throughout the year?
- If you had to say thank you without words, what would it look like?
- How does saying thank you change you?

Vitamins and Minerals:

Give thanks to the LORD, call on his name; make known among the nations what he has done. (Psalm 105:1)

---

1. Bruce E. Johansen, "State Names, Native American Derivations," ABC-CLIO Schools, copyright © 2011, accessed June 6, 2013, http://www.historyandtheheadlines.abc-clio.com/ContentPages/ContentPage.aspx?entryId=1171768&currentSection=1161468&productid=5.

Prune Face

Mealtime Prayer:
Thank God for His goodness, His mercy, and His forgiveness. Ask Him to help you forgive those who have offended you.

Appetizer:
Place a plum and a prune on a plate. Did you know that a prune is a shriveled-up plum? How are they alike? How are they different? How do you think a plum turns into a prune?

Main Course:
Have one person smile while another person frowns. How are their faces different? How is a smiling face like a plum? How is a frowning face like a prune? Which do you prefer to look at? Why?

Some people who are angry walk around with shriveled-up prune faces. The Bible tells us to get rid of our anger on the very same day that we become angry. How can we get rid of anger and turn from a prune to a plum? Forgiveness is a key to losing anger and gaining joy.

Table Talk:
- Would you rather be a prune face or a plum face?
- Why should we forgive others? How do we do that?
- Why does God forgive us when we sin?

Vitamins and Minerals:
[As Psalm 4:4 says,] "In your anger do not sin": Do not let the sun go down while you are still angry. (Ephesians 4:26)

Give Me a Break

Mealtime Prayer:
Thank God that He loves us and cares about us, and that He wants to help us with our problems.

Appetizer:
Here are some problems to figure out:

Q: What is black and white and has 16 wheels?
A: A zebra on roller skates.
Q: What do you call a mosquito with a tin suit?
A: A bite in shining armor.
Do you know other riddles?

Main Course:
Here are some possible problems: bad hair day, science class, how to get the last drop out of the Coke can, an angry friend. What are two problems you are facing? Come up with a solution for each, such as "Wet your hair and start again." Some problems are harder to solve. Where can you go for help?

The Bible tells us that God loves us and cares about our problems. First Peter 5:7 says, "Cast all your anxiety on him because he cares for you." What does that mean?

Table Talk:
- How do we give our problems to God?
- How does doing that help us feel better?
- Name two ways you can discover God's answer to your problems.

Vitamins and Minerals:
[Jesus said,] "Come to me, all you who are weary and burdened, and I will give you rest." (Matthew 11:28)

What's New?

Mealtime Prayer:
Thank God for His never-ending love, His faithfulness, and His forgiveness.

Appetizer:
After everyone finds his or her place at the table, get up and have everyone switch places. How do you feel sitting in a different place?

Main Course:
Did you ever have a best friend who found a new best friend or who moved away?

Did you ever look forward to being with someone, and then that person changed his or her plans? How did you feel? Why are some changes bad?

Name some changes that could happen in your life. When can changes be good? When can staying the same be good? When can it be bad?

With God, things never change. The Bible says He is always the same.

Table Talk:
- What are some things about God that you hope will never change?
- How does the fact that God never changes make you feel?
- How would your life be different if God changed from day to day?

Vitamins and Minerals:
Jesus Christ is the same yesterday and today and forever. (Hebrews 13:8)

Tastes Like Chicken

Mealtime Prayer:

Jesus often prayed alone (Matthew 14:23). Have each person pray silently for his or her food.

Appetizer:

Have you heard that frog legs taste just like chicken? Have you ever eaten frog? Frogs may taste that way, but a chicken is a chicken and a frog is a frog! What are three differences between the two?

Main Course:

People sometimes confuse other things. Have you heard someone say, "The Bible is a good storybook, but real life is different"? How would you respond? History and archaeology offer proof of the realness of the Bible. Also, you could use certain Bible verses to show the truth about the Bible. (Second Timothy 3:15–17 is one reference. The prophecies about Jesus, such as Isaiah 53:4–6 or John 1 are some others. Can you think of another?)

Since the Bible is real and true, it's like an instruction manual for life.

Table Talk:

- Why is it important to make a habit of reading God's Instruction Manual? What time could you set aside each day to do this?
- What real stories in the Bible help you today?

Vitamins and Minerals:

Do your best to present yourself to God as one approved, a workman who does not need to be ashamed and who correctly handles the word of truth. (2 Timothy 2:15)

God Is Berry Good

Mealtime Prayer:

*Lord, I pray today that at this meal, we will fellowship with You.
Amen.*

Appetizer:

Q: When does 1 + 1 + 1 = 1?

A: When Father + Son + Holy Spirit = God.

Main Course:

To show an example of the Trinity, bring out a fruit pie. Slice the pie into three pieces. Point out how the three pieces are separate but are all part of the whole. The insides may run together, but they are still different pieces. How is this pie like God? (The Father, Son, and Holy Spirit are three-in-one!)

Table Talk:

- Read Luke 10:21. What is one of the Father's roles?
- Read John 14:26. What is one of the Holy Spirit's roles?
- Read John 3:16–17. What is Jesus' main role?
- How does each person of the Trinity help you in daily living?

Vitamins and Minerals:

[Jesus said,] "Make disciples of all nations, baptizing them in the name of the Father and of the Son and of the Holy Spirit." (Matthew 28:19)

Heavenly Preparations in Progress

Mealtime Prayer:

Close your eyes and imagine a meal set before you in heaven. Thank God for the food He's given you today and the food He's preparing for you in heaven.

Appetizer:

Did you know that truffles are a small, rare fungus that grows close to the roots of trees in woodlands? Dogs and hogs hunt out truffles because they are able to sniff them out underground. Truffles are used in fancy gourmet cooking. They sell for as much as $3,600 a pound. How do you think even expensive truffles would compare to food in heaven?

Main Course:

Read John 14:2–6. Where was Jesus going? What was He going to do? Jesus has been preparing a place for us in heaven for thousands of years. Can you imagine how wonderful it will be? God will give us homes, food, and cities that dwarf the luxury of any earthly truffle.

Table Talk:

- Who is "the way" to heaven? What does that mean?
- What does it mean that Jesus is "the truth"?
- What does it mean that Jesus is "the life"?
- In your own words, how would you describe heaven? What special preparations do you think Jesus is making for you there?

Vitamins and Minerals:

Jesus replied, "Where I am going, you cannot follow now, but you will follow later." (John 13:36)

---

1. Lesley Stahl, "Truffles: The Most Expensive Food in the World," *60 Minutes*, January 8, 2012, http://www.cbsnews.com/8301-18560_162-57354702/truffles-the-most-expensive-food-in-the-world/.

Adam's Apple

Mealtime Prayer:

Lord, help me to be content with the fact that You will never leave me or forsake me.

Appetizer:

Q: At what time of the day did God create Adam?

A: A little before Eve.

Main Course:

On your body, where is your Adam's apple located? Your Adam's apple is part of your voice box. It was named after Adam's "apple" (or fruit) in the Bible, but only because the shape looks like a small, rounded apple under the skin. (Most girls don't have Adam's apples.)[1] Read Genesis 2:17 and Genesis 3:4–5. What did God say would happen if Adam ate from the Tree of Knowledge of Good and Evil? What was different about what the serpent told Eve?

Satan was tricky. He tempted Eve by making her think she was missing out on something special, and that God was wrong. Where does Satan's way always lead?

Table Talk:

- What things does Satan make you feel you're missing out on? How does he try to convince you God is wrong? What happens when you believe him?
- What can you do when Satan tempts you?

Vitamins and Minerals:

[Jesus said,] "Watch and pray so that you will not fall into temptation. The spirit is willing, but the body is weak." (Matthew 26:41)

---

1. Dr. Mary L. Gavin, ed., "What's an Adam's Apple?" KidsHealth, August 2010, http://kidshealth.org/kid/talk/qa/adams_apple.html.

Tomato Face!

Mealtime Prayer:

Tonight, as you thank God for your food, also ask Him to help you be obedient.

Appetizer:

Did you know that when tomatoes were first brought to Europe from the New World in the sixteenth century, some people believed they brought good luck,[1] so they made stuffed fabric pincushions to look like them?[2] Tomatoes don't really bring good luck, but they are useful for other things. Name a few.

Main Course:

What kinds of things give you a "tomato" (red) face because of embarrassment? For example, have you ever gotten into trouble in front of your friends? Did your face turn bright red like a tomato? All of us mess up once in a while, but God can help. Repentance means turning away from sin, toward obedience. Is there anything you need to turn away from?

Table Talk:

- What does God do when you repent? How does that feel?
- How can reading the Bible help you to stay out of trouble?
- Read Proverbs 11:17; 19:23; and 28:14. How is that type of help sure to keep your face from turning red?

Vitamins and Minerals:

Is any one of you in trouble? He should pray. Is anyone happy? Let him sing songs of praise. (James 5:13)

---

1. Jackelin J. Jarvis, "The Precious Tomato," LifeinItaly.com, accessed June 6, 2013, http://www.lifeinitaly.com/food/tomatoes.asp.
2. April Mohr, "Why Are Pincushions Frequently Made to Resemble Tomatoes?" *Threads*, February 28, 2012, http://www.threadsmagazine.com/item/23383/why-are-pincushions-frequently-made-to-resemble-tomatoes.

Choices, Choices

Mealtime Prayer:
Sometimes prayer is asking for help. Ask God to help you choose what is right.

Appetizer:
Place a piece of candy under one of three overturned cups. Mix them up; then give everyone a chance to guess which cup has the candy under it. Whoever guesses correctly gets to eat the candy. (Yes, before dinner!) How did wanting that candy help you choose? Would you make the same choice if a spider was under the cup? Why or why not?

Main Course:
After Moses died, Joshua led the people of Israel to the Promised Land. But they soon picked up bad habits from their neighbors and made poor choices. Read Joshua 24:13–15.

What difference would their choice make? Should this have been a difficult choice? What things keep us from choosing God?

Table Talk:
- What was the simplest choice you made today? The most difficult?
- If Joshua asked you his question, what would you choose? Why?
- Have you ever had to choose God's ways over the ways of someone else? What happened?

Vitamins and Minerals:
I have chosen the way of truth; I have set my heart on your laws. (Psalm 119:30)

Good from Bad

Mealtime Prayer:
Ask God to give you patience and to trust Him during difficult times.

Appetizer:
Have everyone taste a spoon of cottage cheese. How does it taste? Do you like it? Some people don't like the flavor, but cottage cheese is actually good for you. It's full of nutrients and proteins.

Main Course:
Think of a time when you thought something was going to be bad for you, but it turned out to be good. What happened? What did you learn?

The Bible tells of a boy named Joseph who was thrown into a pit by his brothers and was later sold as a slave and taken to Egypt. What do you think Joseph thought about that? How would you have responded? (See Genesis 41.) How did this bad thing become good?

Joseph trusted God and kept on doing what was right. When his brothers came to Egypt to get food, they were afraid of Joseph. But Joseph wasn't mad. He said, "You intended to harm me, but God intended it for good" (Genesis 50:20).

Table Talk:
- When things don't go the way you want them to, how do you feel?
- How easy is it to trust that God loves you right then?
- What can help you trust God's love in those times?
- Name two ways you can be like Joseph.

Vitamins and Minerals:
We know that in all things God works for the good of those who love him, who have been called according to his purpose. (Romans 8:28)

A Garden of Goodness

Mealtime Prayer:

For rosy apples, juicy plums, and yellow pears so sweet,
For hips and haws and bush and hedge, and flowers at our feet,
For ears of corn all ripe and dry, and colored leaves on trees,
We thank You, heavenly Father God, for such good gifts as these.[1]

Appetizer:

Did you know that lettuce is in the same plant family as dandelions and daisies,[2] and peanuts are in the same family as bean and peas, not nuts?[3] These foods are all good for you! (Unless you have a peanut allergy.)

Main Course:

Plant a "garden of goodness" in your life today: First, plant Ps: patience, peace, and prayer. Next, plant squash: squash gossip; squash anger; and squash meanness. Then plant lettuce: lettuce love the Lord; lettuce be gentle; lettuce be joyful; lettuce be self-controlled.

Table Talk:

- What other "vegetables" can you plant in your life?
- What other "peas" can you come up with? Squash? Lettuce?
- How do these things "feed" others?

Vitamins and Minerals:

[Jesus said,] "By their fruit you will recognize them." (Matthew 7:20)

---

1. Attributed to Jack Miffleton.
2. The Seed Site, "Asteraceae: The Daisy Family," accessed June 6, 2013, http://theseedsite.co.uk /asteraceae.html.
3. The Peanut Institute, "Peanut Facts," © 2013, accessed June 6, 2013, http://www.peanut-institute .org/peanut-facts/.

Watch Them Jiggle

Mealtime Prayer:
God wants our faith to be strong and unmovable like Him. Look around and find something solid, such as the table or the walls. (Hopefully not your food!) As you pray for your meal, ask God to make your faith solid like that item.

Appetizer:
Did you know that you can grow seeds in Jell-O and observe their root structures? Did you know that a teaspoon of Jell-O dissolved in a cup of warm water makes hair gel? (Please get parental permission before attempting this!) What is your favorite flavor of Jell-O? Why?

Main Course:
How can people without God be like jiggly Jell-O? How does lack of belief affect a person's emotions? A person's life? Remember, Jell-O may be great for dessert, but we have Someone much more solid to put our faith in.

Table Talk:
- How does knowing that God is always "solid" help you to stand firm (for example, He is always true, so I'll tell the truth)?
- What can we tell others about God's solidness (for example, God always hears our prayers)?
- How does having solid belief in God affect you?

Vitamins and Minerals:
Every good and perfect gift is from above, coming down from the Father of the heavenly lights, who does not change like shifting shadows. (James 1:17)

Eating It Up

Mealtime Prayer:
Thank God for the many meals around the world.

Appetizer:
Did you know that the Jews in Jesus' day obeyed strict
laws, which told them what to eat and how to dress?
But Jesus didn't look at the outside; He looked at the
heart. Peter was willing to break the laws of the Jews to share Jesus.
When would you have to break a law to share Jesus?

Main Course:
Peter was one of Jesus' disciples. As a Jew, Peter couldn't eat certain animals,
such as pigs—until he had a vision from God. Read Acts 10:11–15. What did
this vision tell Peter? Later, Peter realized that God was talking about different
people as well as different food (verses 34–35).

Before Jesus came to earth, God mainly worked through His chosen people, the Jews. After the vision, Peter knew that God wanted all people to receive
the good news that Jesus' death was for everyone. Why was this so important?

Table Talk:
- Why does God care about all people, not just those of a certain faith?
- What social "laws" (such as, don't eat with the unpopular kid) might
  need to be broken? Why?
- Name three people in your neighborhood or school whom God loves
  just as much as He loves you. How can you share Jesus with them?

Vitamins and Minerals:
God does not show favoritism but accepts men from every nation. (Acts
10:34–35)

I Smell Trouble!

Mealtime Prayer:

Thank God for helping your family get through a difficult time.

Appetizer:

Have everyone tell about the worst thing they ever smelled.

Main Course:

Have everyone close their eyes. Have each person take a turn at saying the name of something that has a strong, pleasant smell. Take at least 20 seconds or so for everyone to imagine they can smell it.

Repeat this exercise, only now have each person say the name of something that smells bad. It's okay—be silly, mention someone's feet if you want!

Did you ever hear someone say, "I smell trouble"? What does that mean?

Table Talk:

- Have you ever been in a situation where you thought you could "smell" trouble? How? What did you do?
- How can certain people "smell" like trouble? Explain a time when you met someone who "smelled" of trouble. What happened?
- What do your friends "smell" like? How can their smell rub off on you? What kind of smell do you want to have?

Vitamins and Minerals:

Do not be yoked together with unbelievers. For what do righteousness and wickedness have in common? Or what fellowship can light have with darkness? (2 Corinthians 6:14)

Aloha!

Mealtime Prayer:
Pray this poem that Christian Hawaiians sang hundreds of years ago:
Majestic sweetness sits enthroned,
On my Redeemer's brow,
His head with radiant glories crowned,
His lips with grace overflow.

Appetizer:
Did you know that in the nineteenth century, more than 900 Christian hymns were translated into Hawaiian?[1] Some are still sung today. Favorite foods of a luau are *laulau* (pork cooked in leaves), fish, and *ahupia* (coconut-milk custard).

Hawaiian Luau:
Before your meal, string popcorn, and tie the strings into necklaces for mock leis. Prepare fish for dinner. After your meal, do the limbo under a broomstick.

Aloha! Hawaiian leis are given to show appreciation and friendship. Today, it's popular for leis to be made of flowers, leaves, and vines. How would it feel to wear a lei like that? What would it smell like? The Bible speaks of garlands of beauty. Read Proverbs 1:8–10 and/or 4:8–10. Why is obedience beautiful?

Table Talk:
- What have you done today that adorns your neck with beauty?
- If you could visit Hawaii, what new thing would you try?
- Why do you think translating hymns into Hawaiian was important to the first missionaries?

Vitamins and Minerals:
[Wisdom] will set a garland of grace on your head and present you with a crown of splendor. (Proverbs 4:9)

---

1. "Hawai'i Aloha," Huapala.org: Hawaiian Music and Hula Archives, © 2012, accessed June 6, 2013, http://www.huapala.org/Hawaii/Hawaii_Aloha.html.

Fun with Fondue

Mealtime Prayer:

Thank You, Lord, for Your bountiful blessings. May my every action, great or small, be acceptable to You this night. Amen.

Appetizer:

Did you know that Jesus was baptized in the Jordan River? That is the same river that Elisha told Naaman to dip in! What other Bible stories happened at the Jordan River? (The Israelites crossed it to take Jericho, Joshua 3—4; Elijah parted it with his cloak, 2 Kings 2.)

Main Course:

Serve fondue tonight. If you don't want to serve a whole fondue meal, try a dessert fondue—dip fresh fruit and chunks of pound cake into melted chocolate.

Before you begin the meal, read 2 Kings 5. Naaman thought dipping in the water was too simple, but what did God want Naaman to discover? What's more important, obeying God in big things or obeying Him in small things? Why?

Each time you dip your fondue tonight, mention one simple thing you can do for God, such as holding the door open for someone at the store or waving to a neighbor. How many different ideas did you come up with?

Table Talk:

- Were there magical powers in the river that healed Naaman? How do you know?
- Who healed Naaman? Why?
- What did Naaman prove by following God's commands?

Vitamins and Minerals:

[Naaman] said, "Now I know that there is no God in all the world except in Israel." (2 Kings 5:15)

Pears and Pairs

Mealtime Prayer:
(Tune: "Yankee Doodle")
> *We thank You, Lord, for daily bread, for rain and sunny weather.*
> *We thank You, Lord, for this our food, and that we are together.*

Appetizer:
How do you and your best friend make a great "pear" (pair)?

Main Course:
Invite a friend for dinner. Serve things that "go together," such as peanut butter and jelly, macaroni and cheese, or corn bread and chili. Fix bananas and pears for dessert.

The best way to ripen pears is to seal them in a plastic bag with a couple of ripe bananas, leaving them at room temperature. The bananas help the pears ripen quickly and evenly. Like pears, we need buddies. Why are buddies important? Read these verses that tell why Jesus is such a good friend.
- Proverbs 18:24: What type of example is Jesus?
- Hebrews 13:5–6: Will Jesus ever move away? How can Jesus help you?

Table Talk:
- What makes a good friend? What are three reasons that Jesus is the best Friend of all?
- How does your friend help you become a better person? How will Jesus help you become the person God designed you to be?

Vitamins and Minerals:
There is a friend who sticks closer than a brother.
(Proverbs 18:24)

Pizza Party

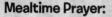

Mealtime Prayer:

Lord, thank You for the variety of foods You have blessed me with. Thank You also for the different parts of my life. May my body, mind, and soul belong to You today. Amen.

Appetizer:

Did you know that we eat three billion pizzas every year? The average American eats 46 slices of pizza a year![1] How many does your family eat in one month?

Main Course:

Order or make everyone's favorite—pizza! Decorate your house like an old-fashioned pizza parlor. Play 1950s music.

Just like a pizza, how is your life split into different sections? What are those different sections (home, school, friends, recreation, church, sports, etc.)? God wants to be involved in every part. Why? Think of one way that God can help in each part of your life.

Table Talk:

- If your life were a pizza with slices, how many slices would you say belong to God?
- Which slices of your life are hardest to let Him control?
- Which slices do you enjoy the most?

Vitamins and Minerals:

[Jesus said,] "Love the Lord your God with all your heart and with all your soul and with all your strength and with all your mind." (Luke 10:27)

---

1. Statistic Brain, "Pizza Statistics," June 18, 2013, http://www.statisticbrain.com/pizza-statistics/.

Human Play Dough

Mealtime Prayer:

Thank You, Lord, that You are shaping us into the kind of people You want us to be. Thank You for sending Jesus to be our example. Amen.

Appetizer:

Q: About 267 of these are born every minute of every day.[1] We come in all different shapes, sizes, and colors. What are we?

A: Human beings.

Main Course:

Parents need to make the following recipe ahead of time.

Peanut Butter Play Dough: 1 cup creamy peanut butter; 1 cup corn syrup; 1¼ cup confectioner's sugar; 1¼ cup dry powdered milk. Mix until smooth and well blended. Add a little more powdered milk if it's sticky.

Have each person mold a person or animal out of the play dough. Guess what it is. Reshape it into something else and guess again. When you're done, eat and enjoy.

Table Talk:

- How are we are like play dough to God? Why?
- What kind of people do you think God wants to mold us into? Why? Name personality traits He'd like His people to have.
- What traits or character qualities do you want God to "shape" in you? What are some ways He might do that?

Vitamins and Minerals:

"O house of Israel, can I not do with you as this potter does?" declares the LORD. "Like clay in the hand of the potter, so are you in my hand, O house of Israel." (Jeremiah 18:6)

---

1. Sam Roberts, "World Population Forecast to Top 7 Billion in 2011," *New York Times*, July 29, 2010, http://www.nytimes.com/2010/07/30/world/30population.html?_r=0.

Got the Goose Bumps?

Mealtime Prayer:

Lord, thank You for Your love and comfort when we feel afraid.

Appetizer:

Q: Why do basketballs and footballs have goose bumps but not baseballs?

A: Basketball and football are played in the winter.

Main Course:

Most people call them goose bumps, but some call them goose flesh or goose pimples. Animals get them too. Ever see a cat or dog when its hair is standing on end?

Besides getting goose bumps, what other ways can our bodies react when we feel frightened? How do those reactions help us? Fear is not always a bad thing. Give some examples of how fear can keep us from harm.

Think of times we are afraid of things that we shouldn't be. Describe a time this happened. For example: Were you were afraid to try something new (like tryouts for the soccer team), but later you were glad you had the courage to overcome your fear?

Table Talk:

- Name other situations or experiences that might make us fearful. For example, going on a long trip, going to a new school, or starting a new job.
- What should you do when you feel afraid? Discuss things that might help you feel better. How can God help you when you are afraid?

Vitamins and Minerals:

When I am afraid, I will trust in you. (Psalm 56:3)

The Spittin' Image

Mealtime Prayer:

Dear Lord, thank You for creating us in Your image. Thank You for sending Jesus to help us see who You are.

Appetizer:

Q: Why do identical twins look the same while other twins do not?

A: Identical twins come from the same egg, while fraternal twins come from separate eggs.

Main Course:

Take a good, hard look at the family members seated around the table with you. In what ways do you look the same? In what ways are you different?

Table Talk:

- Why do family members often resemble one another?
- Christians are all part of God's family. In what way do Christians resemble one another? Think of your Christian friends. How do you resemble each other?
- Christians are also God's children. In what ways do we resemble God? In what ways are we different from Him?
- Name five ways we can become more like God in His character, actions, or attitude.

Vitamins and Minerals:

Then God said, "Let us make man in our image, in our likeness." (Genesis 1:26)

You Are Here

Mealtime Prayer:

Dear Lord, thank You for showing us the way back home to You through Jesus. Please help us to always stay on the right path.

Appetizer:

How many different modes of transportation starting with the letter *B* can you name in 30 seconds? Go! (Sample answers: boat, bicycle, balloon, bulldozer, blimp, bull)

Main Course:

If you have a globe, get someone to spin it. (Or use an atlas.) Have someone else close his or her eyes and stop the globe with one finger. (If you don't have a globe, use a map.) Where did the person's finger land? How far away is it from where you live? If you couldn't fly, how many different modes of transportation would you have to use to reach the location? How long do you think the trip would take? If you didn't have a map, how might you find your way to that location?

Table Talk:

- If life is a journey, what do you think the destination is? Why?
- How can you get there? How long will it take? What might you face along the way?
- Where might you look to find a map for life? How would this map help you?

Vitamins and Minerals:

You have made known to me the path of life; you will fill me with joy in your presence, with eternal pleasures at your right hand. (Psalm 16:11)

Today's Special Is . . .

Mealtime Prayer:

Dear God, please help us to serve one another out of love and consider others' needs and wants, not just our own.

Appetizer:

Describe the funniest experience you've ever had in a restaurant (for example, spilled food, mixed-up order, funny comment, etc.).

Main Course:

Parents need to prepare ahead of time. Have one of the children dress up as a waiter or waitress and then eat before the family comes to the table. When everyone is seated, the waiter or waitress walks in with the menu on a paper and says, "Today's special is . . . " He or she reads the menu, asks for orders, and then serves the food. Ask those around the table: What is the best and worst service you've ever had?

Table Talk:

- What kind of attitude do you need to have toward people you're serving in order to serve them well? How can you get that attitude?
- Jesus was like a servant to His disciples and told us also to serve one another. What does this mean we should do? Give examples.

Vitamins and Minerals:

[Jesus said,] "For who is greater, the one who is at the table or the one who serves? Is it not the one who is at the table? But I am among you as one who serves." (Luke 22:27)

Halos and Wings?

Mealtime Prayer:

Thank You, Lord, for sending us Your angels to help, protect, and encourage us! Amen.

Appetizer:

What does the Bible say about angels? Answer with true or false.

1. Angels are beings created by God. T or F?
2. Angels do not speak. T or F?
3. Angels are considered God's messengers whose chief business is to carry out His orders in the world. T or F?
4. Jesus has charge over the angels. T or F?

(Answers: 1–T, 2–F, 3–T, 4–T)

Main Course:

Angels are mentioned in the Bible about 300 times. Starting with the youngest, have each person try to remember a Bible story about when an angel (or angels) appeared. Why you think God created angels? If you've heard (or read) about someone who was recently helped by an angel, tell that story.

Some people worship or pray to angels as if they were gods. They aren't. Only God is worthy of our worship.

Table Talk:

- How does it make you feel to know angels are watching over you? Why?
- Why do angels help us? Why do you think God sends His angels to us?

Vitamins and Minerals:

For he will command his angels concerning you to guard you in all your ways; they will lift you up in their hands, so that you will not strike your foot against a stone. (Psalm 91:11–12)

Hats On!

Mealtime Prayer:

Thank You, Jesus, for making us a part of Your family. It is a ROYAL honor! Amen.

Appetizer:

Tonight is Mealtime Hat Night. Everyone must find a special hat to wear during dinner. Try to find a hat that says something about you. If you don't have a hat, borrow one or make one out of fabric, paper, or art supplies.

Everyone got a hat? Okay, now try to guess why each person chose the hat he or she is wearing.

Main Course:

What does each person's hat tell about his or her personality? Some people wear special hats that tell what kind of job they have. See how many types of jobs you can list where people must wear a special hat (for example, chef, construction worker, etc.).

Read the scripture under "Vitamins and Minerals," and then tell what kind of hat we will receive in heaven if we belong to Jesus.

Table Talk:

- What kind of people usually wears crowns?
- What does a crown represent?
- Why would God want to give His people crowns in heaven?
- How does it make you feel knowing that someday you can receive the crown of life? Name three ways you can act worthy of that crown this week.

Vitamins and Minerals:

Blessed is the man who perseveres under trial, because when he has stood the test, he will receive the crown of life that God has promised to those who love him. (James 1:12)

Made to Order

Mealtime Prayer:
Have everyone thank God for something unique about the person on his or her left.

Appetizer:
What are blueprints? How did they get their name? Blueprints are reproductions of an architect's building plans. They were originally made by the reaction of light hitting chemically treated paper. This reaction produced white lines on a blue background. Today, however, blueprints are rarely blue. They are printed just like regular documents.

Main Course:
Imagine you won a contest that gave you the chance to build your dream home. What would it look like? How big would it be? Where would it be located? What special features would you add to it?

If God designed the perfect house for you, what would it be like? How would He know what you wanted?

Table Talk:
- If you had a choice to receive a gift, such as a new house, from your mom, a friend, or a complete stranger, who would you choose? Why?
- Do you think God is interested in your likes and dislikes? Why or why not?
- God is interested in giving us what we need. How should this affect the way we pray?

Vitamins and Minerals:
[Jesus said,] "Your Father knows what you need before you ask him." (Matthew 6:8)

Going in Circles

Mealtime Prayer:

Dear Lord, thank You for this time we can spend eating together and enjoying each other's company. Please help us to make the most of every moment we live.

Appetizer:

If you could pop in and out of time, where would you go first? What would you do once you got there? Why?

Main Course:

Bring a ring-shaped object to the dinner table (for example, a ring, a hula hoop, or a bracelet). If you can't find anything, draw a perfect circle (or as close to perfect as you can get) on a piece of paper. You can do this by tracing a circular object. Pass the object or drawing around the table and let everyone study it carefully. Can anyone find the beginning of the circle? The end? Why or why not?

Table Talk:

- Imagine that the circle is perfect. How is God like a perfect circle?
- God is eternal (without beginning or end). Time is irrelevant to Him. (He can pop in and out of time!) How do you think God's eternal nature affects His ability to answer your prayers?

Vitamins and Minerals:

[Jesus said,] "I am the Alpha and the Omega, the First and the Last, the Beginning and the End." (Revelation 22:13)

Enemies Eyeing
Your Plate

Mealtime Prayer:
Ask God to help you not worry or fear when people hate
you, but to help you love them instead.

Appetizer:
Jonathan disagreed with his father—Saul—at the dinner table. So Saul tried to
kill Jonathan with a spear (1 Samuel 20:30–33). What kind of table manners
would you say Saul had?

Main Course:
Name some people who don't like you. Which people act like enemies to you?
What worries do you have about them? God promised that goodness and love
would follow us. He promised to prepare a table for us in the presence of our
enemies. What does that mean? He promised that our cup would overflow.
What does that mean?

Table Talk:
- Is it right or wrong for Christians to have enemies? Explain your
  answer.
- Why do some people hate Christians?
- How did Jesus say we should act toward people who hate us? Why do
  you think He said that? How can loving others help us?

Vitamins and Minerals:
You prepare a table before me in the presence of my enemies. You anoint my
head with oil; my cup overflows. Surely goodness and love will follow me all the
days of my life. (Psalm 23:5–6)

Spice and Everything Nice

Mealtime Prayer:

Have everyone sniff a jar of cinnamon. Pray, *Lord, help all that we do to be like an offering of sweet-smelling spices to You.*

Appetizer:

Bring spices to the table, particularly cinnamon—cinnamon bark if you have it.

Q: Why do you think cinnamon used to be the most expensive spice on earth?

A: It's aromatic, used to be rare, and came from far away.

If you were a spice, what would you be? Why?

Main Course:

In ancient Israel, cinnamon and other spices arrived in caravans from faraway lands, so they were expensive and valuable. Costly perfumes also came from distant countries. Today, most spices are no longer so expensive, but perfume still is. Bring some bottles of perfume to the table. Let everyone smell them. Which one is your favorite? Incense is made out of perfume and spice. Why do you think the Bible says that some prayers are like incense?

Table Talk:

- Paul said the gift the Macedonians gave him was a "fragrant offering" (Philippians 4:18) like sweet spices. How are gifts and good deeds like sweet-smelling spices?
- Wearing different kinds of perfume can make our bodies smell nice. What different character traits should we have (for example, thankfulness) to make our spirits smell nice?

Vitamins and Minerals:

For we are to God the aroma of Christ among those who are being saved and those who are perishing. (2 Corinthians 2:15)

Not a Peep

Mealtime Prayer:

Lord, help us to listen to others with our eyes and hearts, as well as with our ears. Amen.

Appetizer:

Q: I like to jump high and make loud noises by rubbing parts of my body together, and my ears are located on my knees! Who am I?

A: A cricket.

Main Course:

Have people close their eyes and sit as still as they possibly can for at least one minute. Try to concentrate on any little or big sound you hear. Make mental notes of any sounds that you hear, from both close and far away.

Describe how it felt to stay quiet and just listen without moving. Are there times you find it hard to sit quietly and listen when someone else is talking? Why or why not?

Table Talk:

- What do you think most people like better, talking or listening? Which do you prefer? Why?
- How does it make you feel when you know someone is listening carefully to something you are saying?
- What kind of listener do you think God is? Why?
- How can you be a good listener?

Vitamins and Minerals:

My dear brothers, take note of this: Everyone should be quick to listen, slow to speak and slow to become angry. (James 1:19)

Hey! That's Mine!

Mealtime Prayer:
Have everyone thank God for something that someone recently shared with them.

Appetizer:
Everyone name at least one thing that members of your family share with each other.

Main Course:
Alex Cherney, 14, lived in the former Soviet Union before moving to the United States. His family of four lived in a one-room apartment. "We were all packed in," Alex says. "We used furniture as dividers for our own space." The entire building only had five bathrooms, one for every 12 families.

How do you feel about the amount of space your family lives in? Do you wish you had more? Why or why not?

Table Talk:
- What do you think is the hardest part of sharing things (like a TV, bathroom, toys, or personal items)?
- Describe a time when you found it really hard to share something of yours. How did it make you feel? Why was it hard?
- How do you feel when someone shares with you?
- What kinds of things can you share? Think of something this week that our family can share with others.

Vitamins and Minerals:
Do not forget to do good and to share with others, for with such sacrifices God is pleased. (Hebrews 13:16)

Don't Hide That Heart!

Mealtime Prayer:

Pray that the Lord will give your family honest and loving hearts.

Appetizer:

Play Don't Hide My Heart. Appoint one person to stand a few feet away while the rest of the family is seated around the dinner table. Pass two small candy or paper hearts around under the table. Be sneaky about it so the guesser won't know where the hearts are. When the guesser says, "God sees our hearts," stop passing the hearts. The guesser has two guesses to find the person (or persons) with the hearts.

Main Course:

Sometimes people hide things about themselves, like their feelings. The way we act on the outside doesn't always match what we feel on the inside. When have you tried to hide your feelings? How did it make you feel? Have you ever pretended to be happy when you really felt sad inside? Explain.

Table Talk:

- Why do you think it's hard to always be honest about our feelings?
- Are our feelings still there even when we've hidden them? How do you know?
- What kinds of things do we try to hide from God? Why? How well does it work?
- How does God respond to our secrets? What secrets can you trust Him with this week? Take time each day this week to tell God what is hidden in your heart.

Vitamins and Minerals:

The LORD does not look at . . . the outward appearance . . . the LORD looks at the heart. (1 Samuel 16:7)

Home Sweet Home

Mealtime Prayer:
Take turns thanking God for something in your home.

Appetizer:
   Q: What kind of house weighs the least?
   A: A lighthouse.

Main Course:
For hundreds of years, Abraham's descendants lived in tents, first in Canaan, then in Egypt, then in the desert.
   Describe what you think it would be like to live in a tent year-round. When Jesus was born, many people lived in caves. What would it be like to live in a cave? See how many other types of homes your family can name that people either once lived in or still do. (Examples: apartment, teepee, tree house, long house, trailer, houseboat.)

Table Talk:
   • If you belong to Jesus, He is preparing a room for you in God's house (see "Vitamins and Minerals"). What does that mean?
   • What will God's house be like? How can you find out? Where is it?
   • How will you be able to find your way to God's house?
   • What will your favorite part be?

Vitamins and Minerals:
[Jesus said,] "In my Father's house are many rooms; if it were not so, I would have told you. I am going there to prepare a place for you." (John 14:2)

Hot or Cold?

Mealtime Prayer:

Thank God for something that has to do with temperature. (Examples: cold ice cream, warm showers, snow forts, summer days, campfires, etc.)

Appetizer:

See how much everyone knows about hot food. Answer true or false.

1. While eating a hot pepper, nerve endings in your mouth convince your brain it is experiencing true heat! T or F?
2. All peppers are hot. T or F?
3. Drinking water after eating a hot pepper really helps! T or F?
4. A hot pepper contains 3.5 times as much vitamin C as an orange. T or F?

(Answers: 1–T, 2–F, 3–F, 4–T)

Main Course:

Have you ever been called a "hothead"? When? How about a "cold fish"? When? The words *hot* and *cold* are often used to describe our feelings. Think of other ways you've heard these words describe feelings. (Examples: He acted so cool! Her opinion was lukewarm.)

Table Talk:

- What temperature do you like your hot chocolate? Soda pop? Soup? Is there anything you like lukewarm? What and why?
- What attitude would *lukewarm* would describe?
- How do you think God wants us to feel about our relationship with Him? Hot, cold, or lukewarm? Why? What would each be like?

Vitamins and Minerals:

[The Amen said,] "I know your deeds, that you are neither cold nor hot. I wish you were either one or the other!" (Revelation 3:15)

True North

Mealtime Prayer:
Have family members talk about a part of their lives where they really need direction. Then pray that God would help show them the way.

Appetizer:
Q: If you were lost and didn't have a compass, how could you find your bearings?
A: By observing the sun travel from east to west, by finding the North Star, or by using fixed landmarks that you know (the ocean or a mountain range) as a point of reference.

Main Course:
Place a compass on the table. (If you don't have a compass, just picture one.) Which direction does the needle point? If you turn or shake the compass, what happens to the direction of the needle? Why? Why is it important to know where north is if you're lost in the woods?

Table Talk:
- When we say that people are lost without God, what do we mean?
- How is the Bible like a compass? Where does it lead?
- How can you use the Bible to find your way every day?

Vitamins and Minerals:
Show me your ways, O LORD, teach me your paths; guide me in your truth and teach me, for you are God my Savior, and my hope is in you all day long. (Psalm 25:4–5)

FOCUS ON THE FAMILY®

Welcome to the Family

Whether you purchased this book, borrowed it, or received it as a gift, thanks for reading it! This is just one of many insightful, biblically based resources that Focus on the Family produces for people in all stages of life.

Focus is a global Christian ministry dedicated to helping families thrive as they celebrate and cultivate God's design for marriage and experience the adventure of parenthood. Our outreach exists to support individuals and families in the joys and challenges they face, and to equip and empower them to be the best they can be.

Through our many media outlets, we offer help and hope, promote moral values and share the life-changing message of Jesus Christ with people around the world.

Focus on the Family
MAGAZINES

These faith-building, character-developing publications address the interests, issues, concerns, and challenges faced by every member of your family from preschool through the senior years.

For More
INFORMATION

ONLINE:
Log on to
FocusOnTheFamily.com
In Canada, log on to
FocusOnTheFamily.ca

PHONE:
Call toll-free:
800-A-FAMILY
(232-6459)
In Canada, call toll-free:
800-661-9800

THRIVING FAMILY®
Marriage & Parenting

FOCUS ON THE FAMILY CLUBHOUSE JR.®
Ages 4 to 8

FOCUS ON THE FAMILY CLUBHOUSE®
Ages 8 to 12

FOCUS ON THE FAMILY CITIZEN®
U.S. news issues

Rev. 3/11